Girl Gang

Girl Gang

Pete Johnson

Illustrated by Lucy Su

A & C Black • London

First paperback edition 2000
First published 2000 in hardback by
A&C Black (Publishers) Ltd
35 Bedford Row, London WC1R 4JH

Text copyright © 2000 Pete Johnson
Illustrations copyright © 2000 Lucy Su
Cover illustration copyright © 2000 Kim Harley

ISBN 0-7136-5383-3

A CIP catalogue for this book is available from
the British Library.

Printed and bound in Spain by G. Z. Printek, Bilbao.

Chapter One

It was Saturday afternoon, I'd been allowed to go out shopping on my own. I was sitting on the train home, quite unaware how dramatically my life was about to change. My name, by the way, is Alice.

A girl called Kirsty was in my carriage. She was also in my class at school but she never even said 'Hello' to me. I wasn't surprised.

Then the ticket collector suddenly appeared.

All tickets please.

I found mine. Then I watched Kirsty search for her ticket. The ticket collector waited impatiently.

At school on Monday Kirsty ignored me, as usual. So did practically everyone else. I'm not so much unpopular as invisible. I'd been off school with glandular fever for ages and ages. I'm still not allowed to do games. No one really notices me. Sometimes I feel as if I'm a kind of ghost.

After school I often do my homework in the library. I was leaving to go home when Kirsty rushed past.

If old Sour-Breath comes looking for me, you haven't seen me.

What!?

You haven't seen me!

Then she was gone.

Moments later, old Sour-Breath – or Mr Sawyer, our Geography teacher – came panting up. He wore huge glasses and had greasy, straw-coloured hair. There were certain pupils he always picked on. One of them was Kirsty.

Has Kirsty Webb just gone past?

No, sir.

9

Kirsty didn't answer but she smiled at me for a moment. I noticed four other girls standing on the opposite side of the road. One of them was in my class. I didn't recognise the others.

15

Next morning I opened my Geography book to find a note in there for me. My heart began to thump. It said,

URGENT
MEET ME IN THE PARK
8 O'CLOCK TONIGHT
Kirsty

Chapter Two

I told my mum I was going out with some girls from my class. She immediately looked worried.

Of course she will. She's a sensible girl.

Dad was trying to be nice but I didn't like being called 'sensible'. Still, I suppose I was really. I never got into much trouble, nor did my two younger brothers – though they did their best to look hard.

I walked off towards the park. Lee, the boy living opposite, who I've known forever, spotted me.

Suddenly this puppy came rushing over to us.

Aren't you brilliant!

The spaniel barked and leapt around us. A girl came chasing after her.

I'm so sorry about her. She keeps jumping her lead.

It was Vanessa. She was in my form and came top in just about every subject. She was also very pretty. I'd always envied her. She gave me a friendly smile.

Hi Alice.

This is Lee.

Lee coughed loudly.

He grinned at Vanessa.

Vanessa picked the puppy up.

I think it'd be better carrying her. 'Bye.

Lee stared after Vanessa and her puppy.

Stop drooling, Lee.

I'm not. 'Bye now. Mind how you go!

We'd reached the park.

23

I walked on quickly. The park was dark and silent. I felt really nervous. Then shapes appeared out of the darkness. A group of girls loomed over me. Kirsty stepped forward. She introduced the other girls to me. A girl called Sandra seemed to be the leader. She was in the year above me at school.

All the girls were wearing old bomber jackets, short skirts and platform boots. But they also wore lots of jewellery.

Kirsty beckoned me to follow them.

Come with us, then.

The girls walked either side of me. We came out of the park and into the outskirts of the town. We took over the whole pathway.

A boy tried to get past.

Out of the way, girls!

All the girls turned round and glared at him.
Sandra spoke in a hiss.

Don't ever speak to us like that.
You show us some manners.

No one else tried to pass. Some people looked really
scared of us.

All the girls chatted to me. They asked so many questions: even what kind of music I liked. But I felt they were really interested. I couldn't believe how friendly they were to me. I'd never had so much attention.

Then we reached Arnleys, a shop which never seemed to close. But its owner was a bad-tempered man who was always rude to kids from our school.

We went inside.

I don't want you all loitering about in here. Pick what you want and go.

You're very rude.

Get out of my shop. All of you.

Not before you show some respect.

Sandra leant against this shelf full of tins, then sent them flying to the ground.

Sandra threw some packets of cereal on to the ground. Then other girls began knocking and pushing things too.

He watched us, cowering by his counter. He'd always been so rude and nasty. Now, at last, he was showing us proper respect.

I know your names and I'll be phoning all your parents!

I began to worry. Kirsty looked a bit anxious for a moment too.

He's only bluffing.

He knows if he causes any trouble we'll be back.

We marched down the road. Then, to my amazement, up popped Lee. He was across the road staring at us.

What are you looking at?

Lee never said a word. He watched us for a few moments longer and then vanished as quickly as he'd arrived.

Want to see some more action?

Yes, I would.

Janice Godby is really keen to join us. Now we're going to see if she's ready.

We went up this side street. Janice was waiting. She was in my form. She looked very surprised to see me. She was holding a carrier bag full of apples.

Let's go.

We swarmed through the back gate and hid behind the shed. Then, after a signal, Janice charged towards the greenhouse. Janice took the first apple out of the bag and fired it. A crack appeared on one of the greenhouse windows. There was a whispered cheer. Then everyone joined in. Even me. The greenhouse was bombarded with apples.

Everyone ran off. I could hear a man's voice shouting after us. The others were far away, but I was suddenly exhausted. I didn't think I could run another step.

I tried my hardest. Finally, I caught up with the others in the park. They were all shaking Janice by the hand.

Suddenly Sandra was towering over me.

You must promise not to reveal anything you've seen tonight.

I promise.

Well, we might have some news for you soon.

I watched the girls walk away. A small army. I wondered what the news might be. Were they going to let me be a member? That was such an exciting idea I hardly dared think about it.

Chapter Three

Next day after school Kirsty and Sandra were waiting for me.

39

I was so pleased, I could hardly speak at first. They wanted me to be in such a cool gang.

41

42

She handed me an envelope. Inside was a piece of paper.

Alice: Your assigment is to steal Vanessa Scott's secret diary. You have 7 days to carry out this task. Please destroy this message after you have read it.

It seemed a bit sneaky to me. Especially as Vanessa hadn't actually done them any harm. Still, she was teacher's pet and a big-head.

That was my plan too. That night I had a piece of luck. Lee just happened to go for a walk at the same time as Vanessa was out with her puppy. I went over to them. I bent down and patted the puppy.

50

Next day the gang said I could meet up with them down the park. I rolled over the top of my skirt. My parents couldn't believe their eyes.

Alice, what have you done?

This isn't like you.

But it was. I wasn't as nice and sensible as they thought. Now I was someone much more interesting.

Chapter Four

Next day I went round to Vanessa's house.

It was huge, practically a mansion. I felt so jealous of her living here. She seemed really pleased to see me. We played with Jess for a while. Then she showed me her other pets: a cat, two rabbits and a tank full of fish.

57

We went upstairs to her bedroom. She took the diary out of the little drawer of her dressing table. Then she gave it to me. I couldn't believe I was actually holding it.

There's some really embarrassing things in it, like that.

Then Vanessa's mum called her downstairs. I stood there turning the pages. There was more about Matthew Morris, and other embarrassing things too, just what Sandra and Kirsty wanted. All I had to do now was run out of the house with the diary and my assignment was accomplished.

I hesitated. Vanessa wasn't as I imagined. She wasn't stuck-up. I think she was quite lonely really. And she had her problems too.

She came back upstairs.

My mum's a bit depressed. I'm going to have to sit with her for a while.

That's okay.

But come round again soon. No one else has ever read my diary, you know. So I'll have to trust you.

I handed her back the diary.

Next day I decided to see Kirsty and explain why I hadn't carried out the assignment. We met up after school. We walked towards the park.

I was mumbling.

I had the diary in my hand yesterday. But I couldn't take it.

Did someone stop you?

No, it's just Vanessa is different to how we thought.

I tried to explain but Kirsty's eyes had hardened. Suddenly she was gazing furiously at me.

So you speak to her for a few minutes and think you know her better than we do.

That night I hardly slept. In the morning I found another note from Kirsty.

If there's something you really want it's worth doing <u>anything</u> to get it.

Later, I saw Kirsty.

I'll get you the diary tonight.

I know you will. Bring it to school for about eight o'clock tonight. Sandra and I will be waiting for you.

After tea I went round to Vanessa's house again. This time Lee came with me. He said he wanted to see Jess! While he and Vanessa were playing with Jess I slipped upstairs.

I remembered where Vanessa had put the diary. I opened the drawer. There it was. I grabbed it. Now I should run off. I hesitated again. I still hated doing this. I slipped the small bag I had out of my pocket and put the diary inside.

What are you doing?

I whirled round. Lee was watching me.

You're stealing that, aren't you?

I have to.

Why?

I can't explain. Just... just don't tell Vanessa.

She was there in the doorway, looking puzzled and hurt. I didn't say anything. Neither, to my surprise, did Lee. All at once I bolted past them and down the stairs.

Don't tell Vanessa what?

Alice, stop!

I carried on running. I sped out of the house. After a bit I stopped. I had a stitch. But no one seemed to be following me. I struggled to catch my breath.

I'd carried out my assignment. I was a success. Yet, I felt so guilty, as if I'd betrayed Vanessa.

But I don't have a choice, do I?

Chapter Five

Some time later I reached the school. Sandra and
Kirsty jumped out of the shadows.

I waved the diary at them.

Sandra grabbed the diary and started riffling through its pages.

We'll find the really embarrassing bits and photocopy them. I've found a way into the school library.

I stood waiting while Sandra and Kirsty pored over the diary.

Are you sure this was the one?

Positive. Why?

Nothing. We'll go and photocopy this now. You've done well.

So am I in the gang?

You certainly are. We'll tell you what to do next – tomorrow.

71

I left them, my heart still beating very fast. I felt uneasy somehow.

I reached the top of my road. Vanessa and Lee were waiting for me.

73

Suddenly Sandra and Kirsty were looming over us.
I shrank back.

How corny and nice. I thought there was something funny about that diary. That's why we followed you.

All at once Sandra lunged forward and began to punch and kick me. I was completely taken by surprise. Sandra had massive rings on. I felt them scratch against my face.

Vanessa tried to help but one blow from Sandra sent her flying. Lee looked as if he couldn't believe his eyes – he still couldn't bring himself to hit a girl.

In the end it was Kirsty who pulled Sandra off me. I stood there, choking and gasping. I was surprised and grateful.

Thanks.

Kirsty shot me a look of pure hatred.

All you'll ever be is a sad loser.

Lee helped Vanessa to her feet.

Some of the neighbours were coming out, including my mum and dad.

Alice, what's happened to you?

Later, Mum bathed the cuts on my face.

But what was it all about?

Just a misunderstanding. It's all over now.

Next day I went round to Vanessa's house.

If you'd taken my diary you'd be one of the girl gang for sure. Bet you wish you'd stolen it now.

No, I don't. Honestly.

But there were moments when I wished I was in the girl gang.

Sometimes I'd spy on them marching through the park at night. I still liked the way they stood up for themselves. Yet they also picked on people. They said they had good reasons. But I suppose you can always find a reason to bully someone.